The Organ Music of

VOLUME 1
Lenten/Easter

Fred Bock Music Company

ORGAN MUSIC OF INTEREST AND DISTINCTION
from the Fred Bock Music Companies

Fred Bock Music Company ◇ *Gentry Publications* ◇ *H.T. FitzSimons Co.*
Available at your local music dealer

Adagio (from Third Symphony) (JG0657) . . . . .Camille Saint-Saëns/ed. Fred Tulan
All the Things You Are (JG0541) . . . . .Jerome Kern/arr. Billy Nalle
    in the style of a Bach trio sonata
American Folk-Hymn Settings (F0623) . . . . .Jean Langlais
    Amazing Grace, How Firm a Foundation, Battle Hymn, and three more
Ballade for Organ and English Horn (BG0881) . . . . .Leo Sowerby
    (or clarinet, violin, viola)
Century of Czech Organ Music (Vol. 1–F0606/Vol. 2–F0607) . . . . .ed. Karel Paukert
Concert Etude (F0634) . . . . .Anthony Newman
Expressions for Organ (F0624) . . . . .Jean Langlais and Naji Hakim
Folkloric Suite (F0604) . . . . .Jean Langlais
Hymns of Praise and Power (BG0705) . . . . .Frederick Swann
    accompaniments for 15 congregational hymns
Organ Music of Fred Bock—Vol. 1 Six Hymntune Settings (BG0889) . . . . .Fred Bock
    Be Thou My Vision, Morning Has Broken, On Christmas Night, and three more
Organ Music of Leo Sowerby (BG0879) . . . . .Leo Sowerby
    Carillon, Pageant, A Wedding Processional, and two more
Rhumba (JG0544) . . . . .Robert Elmore
Rhythmic Suite *(includes Pavane)* (JG0546) . . . . .Robert Elmore
Thirty Organ Bridges (BG0702) . . . . .Fred Bock
    transition bridges and interludes for service playing
Three Carol Preludes (JG0691) . . . . .Richard Purvis
Toccata on "Christ the Lord Is Risen Today" (BG0634) . . . . .Diane Bish
Trumpet Tune (F0626) . . . . .Jean Langlais
    a work for Trompette-en-Chamade
Variants on Hymntunes for Congregational Singing (BG0629) . . . . .Fred Bock
    last-verse harmonizations on 14 standard congregational hymns

Gentry Publications   H. T. FitzSimons Company

Fred Bock Music Company

Were You There?

Solo : Trumpet
Sw. : Strings
Ch. : Cromhorne
Gt. : 8' Harmonic Flute, Trem.
Ped. : 16' 8' soft, Sw. to Ped.

Traditional
Arranged by Diane Bish

Recit. Style - thoughtful

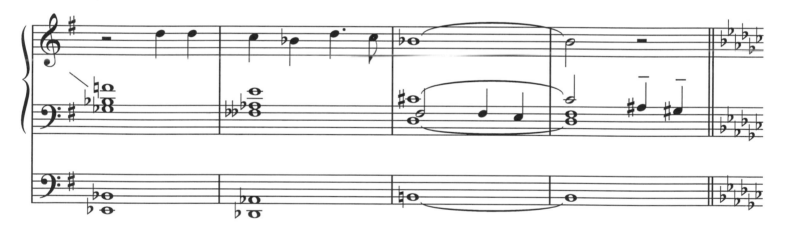

Expressive

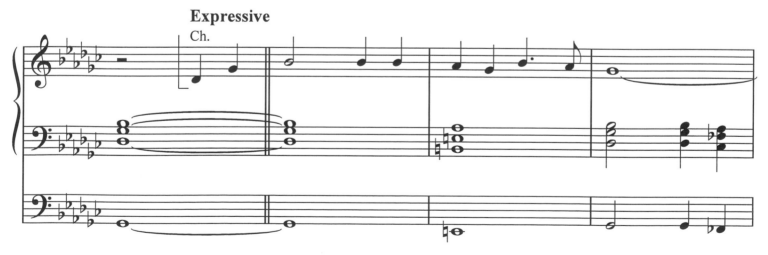

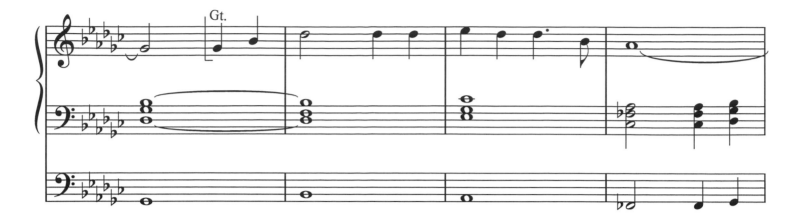

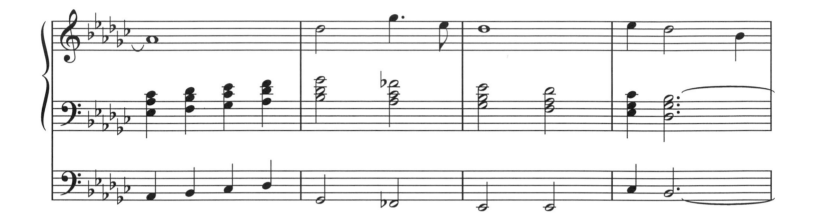

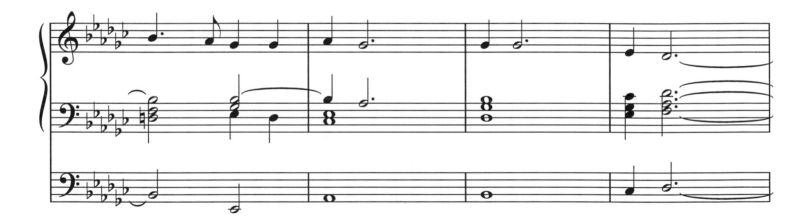

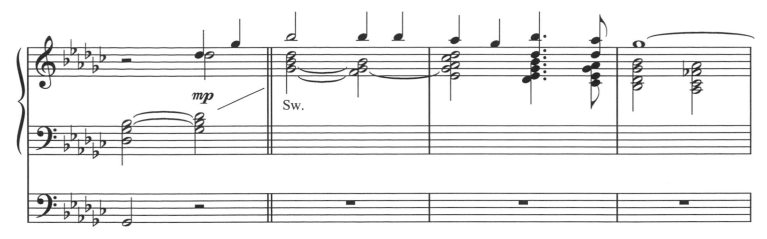

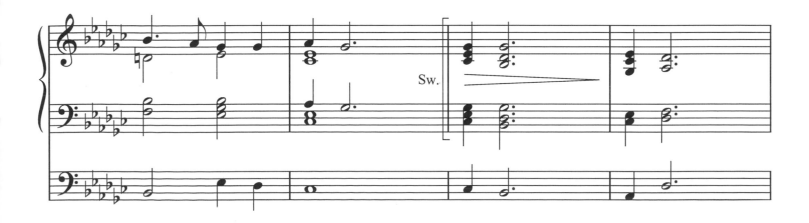

6

+ Foun. 8', 4', 2'
+Mix

+Sw. 16', 8',
4' Reeds

Gt.

Maestoso

ff

Solo
Trumpet

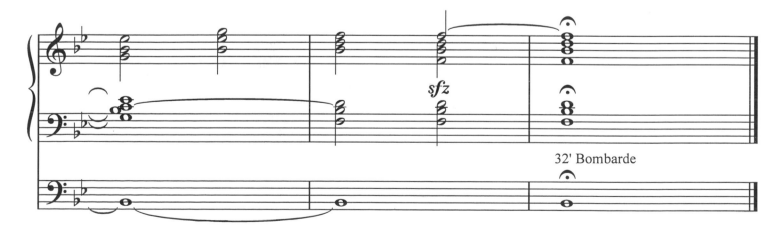

32' Bombarde

When I Survey the Wondrous Cross

Sw. : Strings
Ch. : Clarinet, Tremulant
Gt. : Principals 8′ 4′ 2′
Ped. : Soft 16′, Sw. to Ped.

HAMBURG
Based on Gregorian Chant
Arranged by Diane Bish

Expressive-with movement

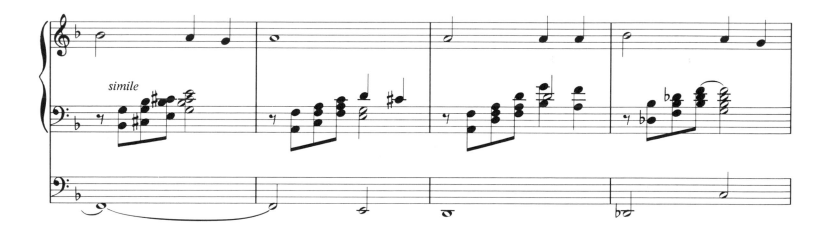

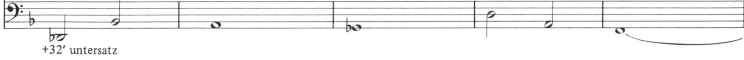

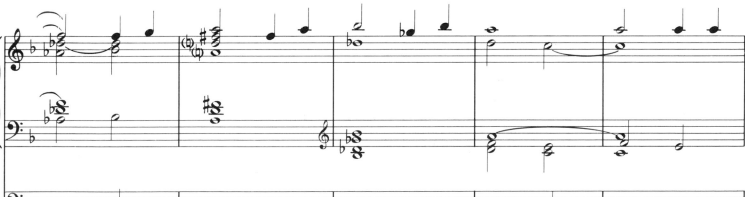

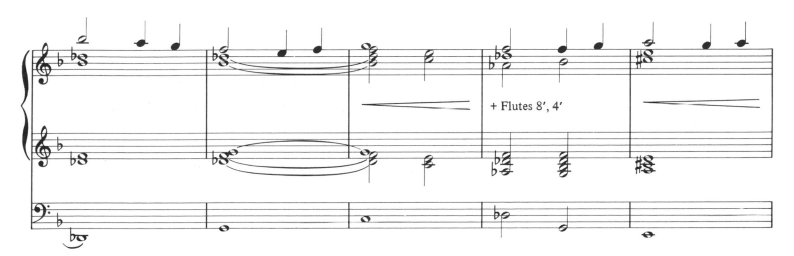

*Do not repeat melody notes

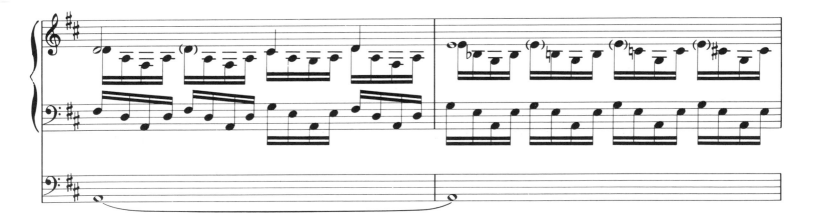

+ Strings 8′, 4′

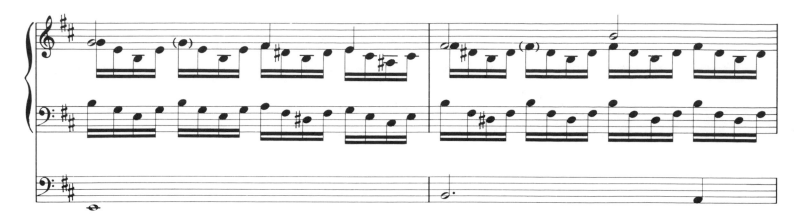

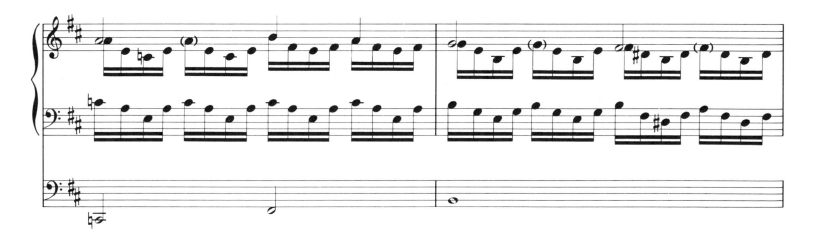

Gt. Foundation, Sw. Ch. to Gt.

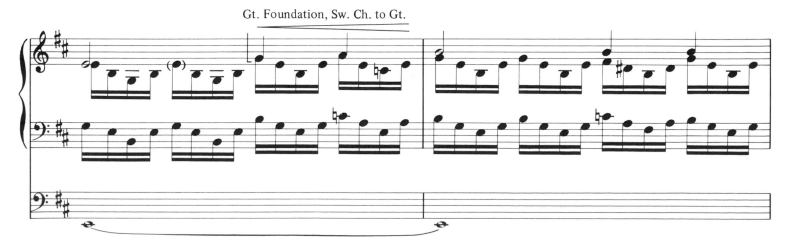

gradual cresc.

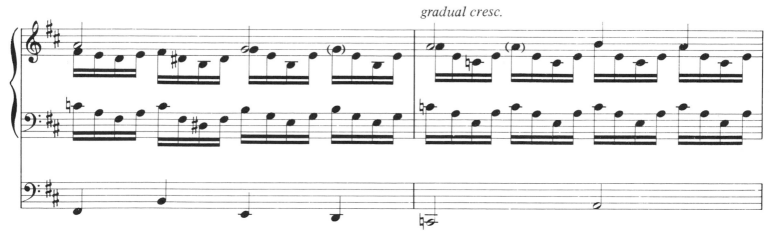

rit.   **A tempo-more briskly**

Full with mix

+32'

+ Sw. 16' 8', 4' reeds

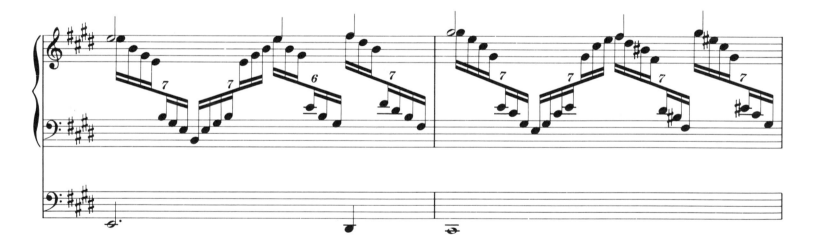

+ 4' coup to Gt.

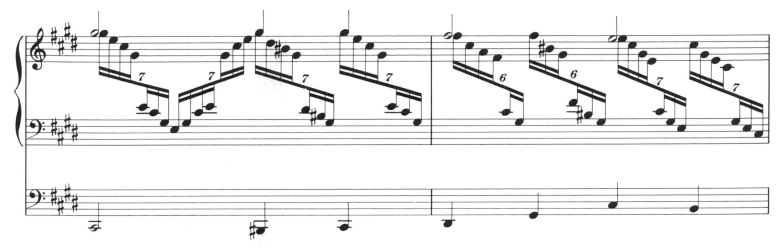

Broaden   *a tempo*

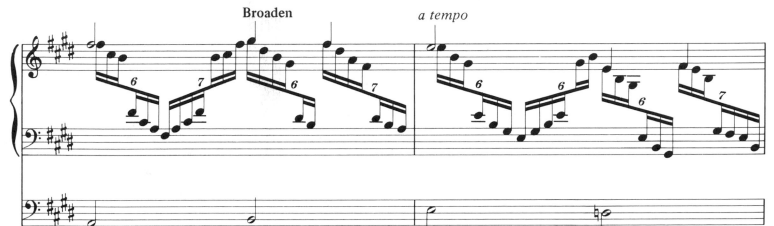

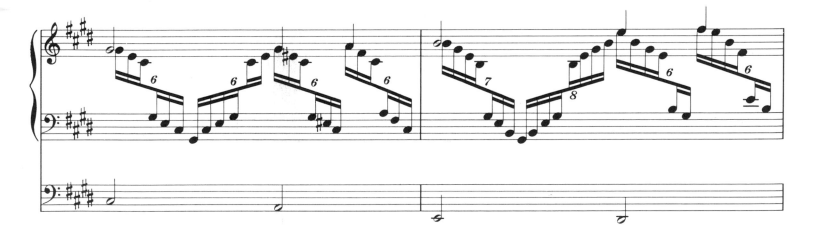

rit.

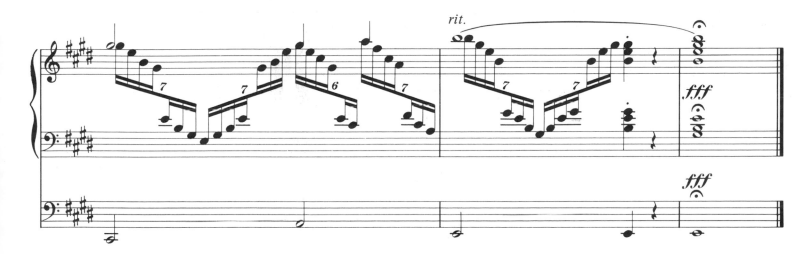

Alas! And Did My Saviour Bleed?

Sw. : Oboe
Ch. : Strings 16' 8' 4'
Gt. : Principle 8' Sw. & Ch. to Gt. 8'
Ped. : 16' 8' Ch. to Ped.

HUGH WILSON
Arranged by Diane Bish

Solemn - Andante

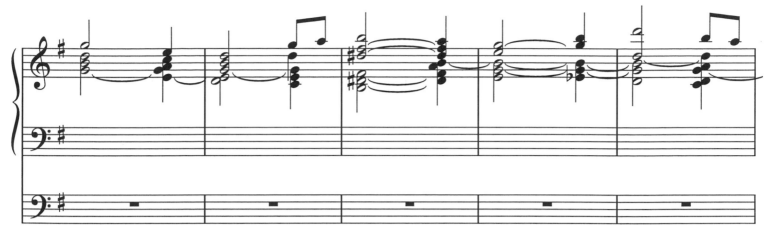

Off Ch. 16'   Sw. (Oboe)

18

Sw. Oboe +
Strings, Flutes

Gt.

Gt.

Gt. Add Sw. 16' 8' 4'
Reeds

Cresc. ped.

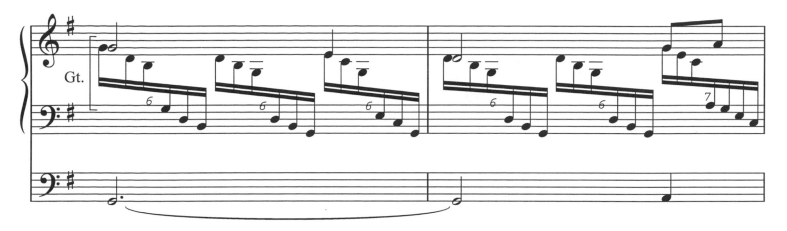

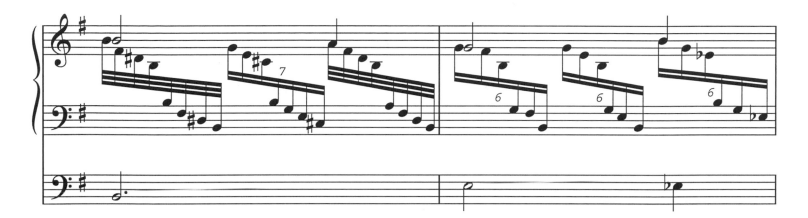

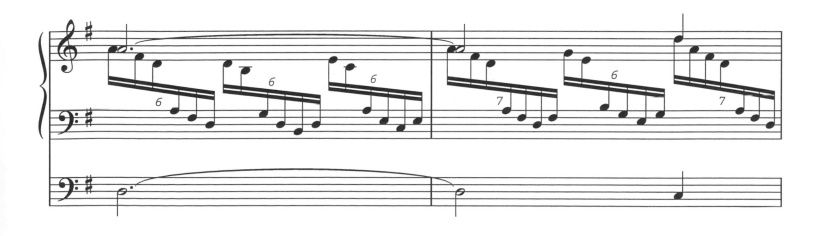

20

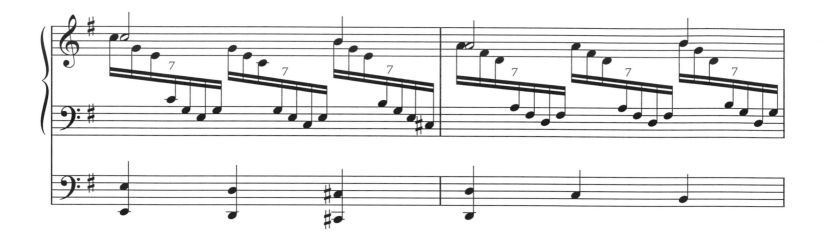

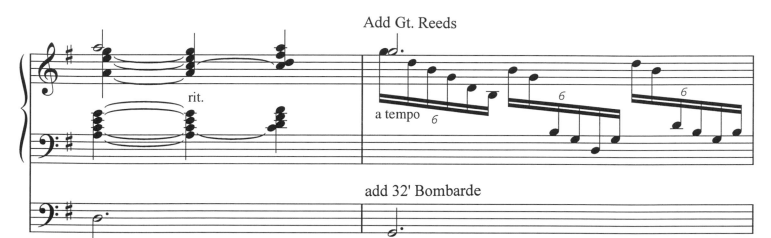

Add Gt. Reeds

rit.

a tempo

add 32' Bombarde

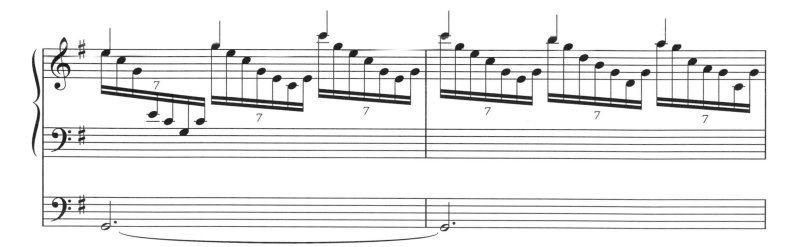

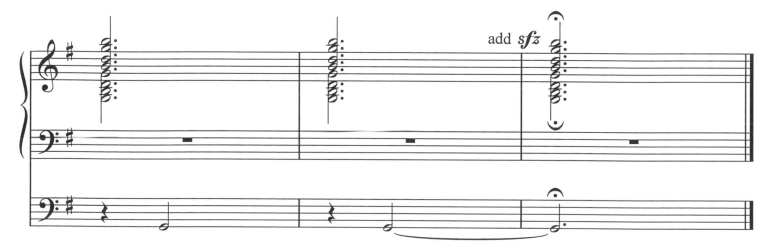

add *sfz*

Toccata on "Christ the Lord is Risen Today"

Sw. : Full, Sw. to Ch. 8′ 4′
Ch. : Full, Couplers 8′ 4′
Gt. : Solo Trumpet
Ped. : Full

EASTER HYMN
"Lyra Davidica"
Arranged by Diane Bish

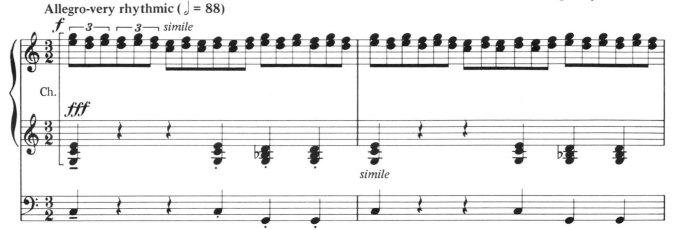

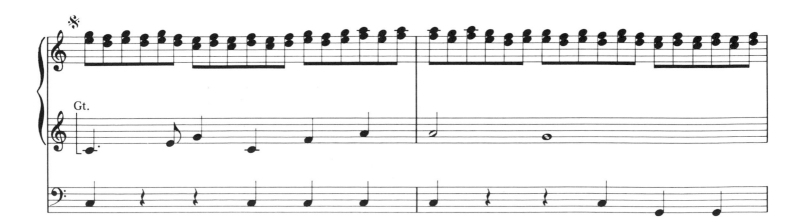

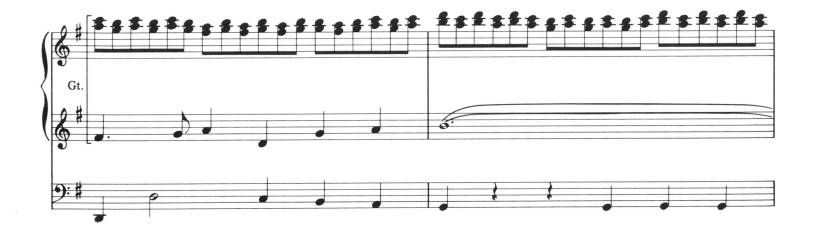

26

2nd time to Coda

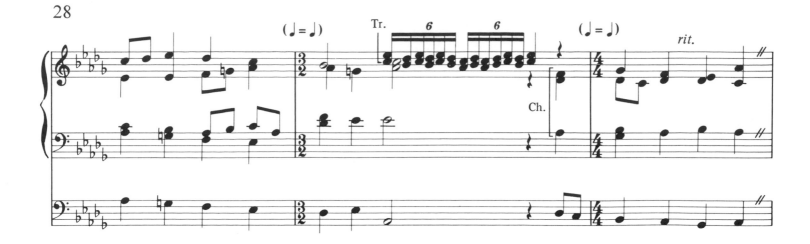

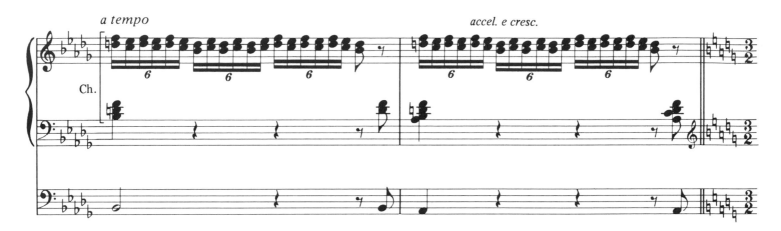

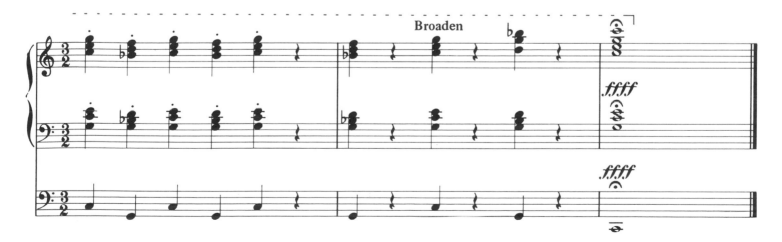

Thine Is the Glory

Sw. : Full: 16' 8' Reeds
Ch. : Full: Sw. to Ch.
Gt. : Trumpet
Ped. : Full

COMPOSER
Arranged by Diane Bish

Majestic

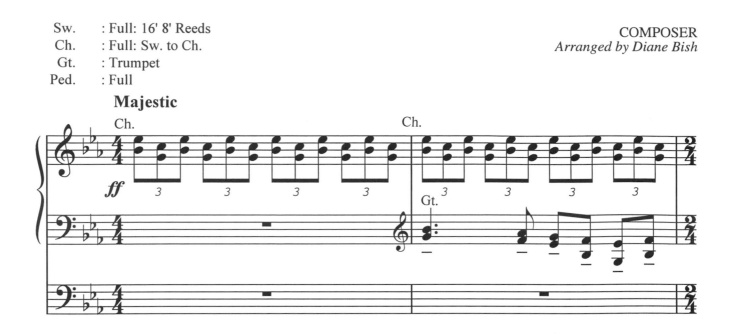

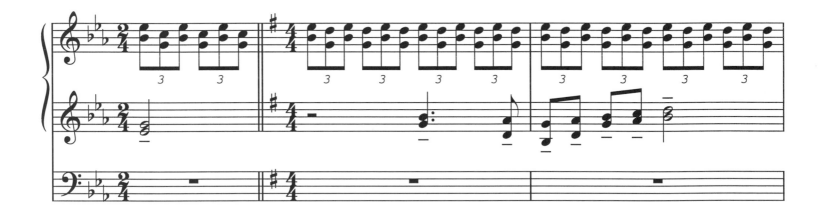

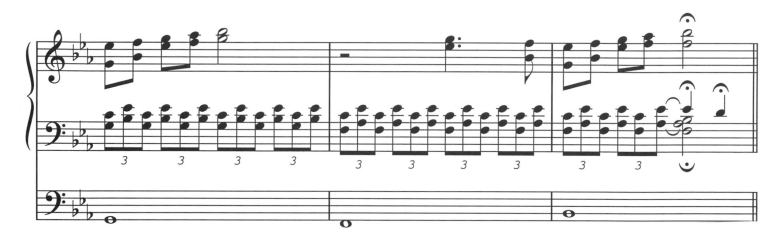

1st time: Full to Sw. Reed
2nd time: Full to mix.

+ Sw. Reeds 16', 8', 4'

Solo Trumpet

fff

Broaden

rit.

+ 32' Bombarde

U.S. $12.95

ISBN 0-634-05610-7

BGK1002

0 73999 09341 4

HL08739260

ISBN - 13: 978 - 1 - 934596 - 46 - 3

51295

9 781934 596463